The Invitation

The Invitation

What life could be if you are open

MOLLY SUTHERLAND

To order additional copies of this book, contact:
Xlibris LLC
0-800-056-3182
www.xlibrispublishing.co.uk
Orders@xlibrispublishing.co.uk
307679

CONTENTS

Preface...11

Chapter One
Is there more than I know?..13

Chapter Two
The depth of God's gift..66

Chapter Three
People's real stories..116

Chapter Four
The one God sent...139

Chapter Five
My story of how all this became real for me.........................148

DEDICATION

This book is dedicated to you!

PREFACE

For over twenty years it has been my privilege to offer classes that enable people to see life in a new way. A way that really helps folk become more fulfilled and more able to enjoy and contribute to this world in which we live for a few years. I have called these classes Resurrected Life Ministry, or RLM. The success we have had has amazed me, so to reach more people I thought I would write this book. So here goes.

Molly Sutherland

CHAPTER ONE

Is There More Than I Know?

This is a book about life
and how we choose to live it.

Are you flying high at the moment,
with the future looking rosy and you feel
in command of the ship?

Or ...

Is life a series of ups and downs,
unpredictable, unstable, with you trying
to find the rudder?

Whichever fits you at the moment,
I invite you to read on.

Have you ever stopped to wonder what is life about and why am I here?

Then this is for you!

What is life all about anyway?

It can seem there is doom, gloom,
depression, doubt, insecurity, fear
all around me.

Am I adding to all this myself through
my own negativity?

What do I give out mostly?
Is it cheerful and uplifting or . . . !?

What if there is another possibility . . .

What if there is a different way to live?

Some people seem different.
Do they know something I don't know?

Are they kidding themselves?
I do not want anything that is not real!

Perhaps it's pie in the sky, you think,
make-believe, unreality.

Better to be depressed and REAL
than float around in a euphoric bubble!

But what if it's the other way round...

What if negativity is actually UNREALITY

and there is ANOTHER way to live?

How about opening our minds to this possibility?

Why not!?

After all, which way we go is always our choice!

But I will not choose what I DO NOT KNOW!

I have to know the choice in order to choose!

I could be missing out on the biggest bargain of all time!

So! OK, are you with me?

Are you willing to hear the choice we have?

If so,

WELCOME ABOARD!

DEEP within all of us, there is an itch to KNOW.

Is this ALL there is?

Is there a God out there?

If there is, what's God like?

Is there something bigger than ME and my understanding?

If God is real, how can I find God?

Quick answer: YOU can't.

Mankind has tried - hence all the religions in the world.

Man cannot connect with God.
We don't have the equipment!

You can't use the internet without a computer or a mobile phone, can you?

Ok! I get the point, so . . .

What is the answer?

You must open your mind to be able to receive it.

Are you ready?

OK! Here it is . . .

God has connected with us!

Our choice is to INVESTIGATE this wonder

Or

DISCARD the possibility.

I Will Investigate This

The consequences of my choice are RECEIVING God's offer of contact

or

deliberately IGNORING God.

To ignore God has very REAL consequences.

Wouldn't you think?

So join me in investigating God's offer of contact.

Let's put ourselves in God's shoes.

How would you contact us if you were God?

How would you, as a human, make
contact with a community of ants?

How could you, as a human person, connect with an ant person?

Wouldn't the best way be to become an ant, hiding your humanity so as not to frighten them?

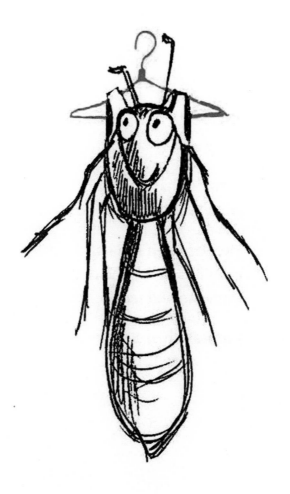

Now . . .

What if that is exactly
what God chose to do!

He was born like us,
lived like us for thirty years,
then showed us

he was more than us.

He was offering us a new way to live
that was far better than how we were living.

He offered to teach us his way
and demonstrated it by
the way he lived life.

He said things that shook our way of thinking.

He helped people in ways no-one had done before.

He showed us how to live life his way.

He offered us friendship and the ability
with his help, to surmount all difficulties.

He opened up communication and relationship between God and humankind that could go as deep as we wanted!

The zip of relationship is in our hands!

No-one had ever opened the door to God.

Now God has opened the door to us.

What an adventure lies before us!

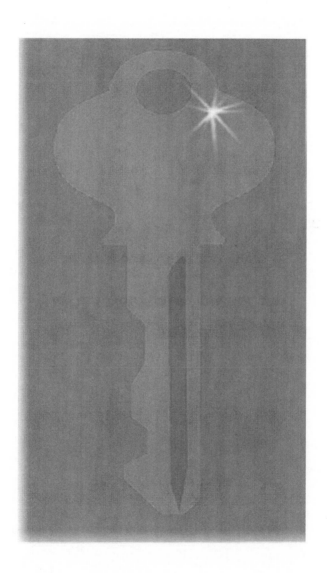

Jumping out of a plane is scary.

But you will never know the thrill unless you first decide to jump!

Why not tell God you want to know more
about his offer of new life!

Could it be that the biggest mistake in
life is to miss God!?

.

Do you want to miss God's bus?

He has made himself available to us.

Let's respond!

Ask him.

Getting Ready To Jump

God, if you are really there and can hear me,
please show me the way you want me to live
and help me live it.

Is it true that you came to show us how to live?

I really need to know!
God, show me please!

YOUR CHOICE

Having read chapter 1, please select your next choice.

Should you wish to know the depth of God's gift.
Then read chapter 2.

You may want to see how other people found God.
Then read chapter 3.

Perhaps you want to know more about the person
Jesus, whom God sent.
Then read chapter 4.

Or maybe you are interested to know how
the author learned all this.
Then join me in chapter 5.

Happy reading!

CHAPTER TWO

The Depth Of God's Gift

The great news is that God has contacted us and invited us into his world.

He has told us why we are here and what future we are each being offered.

He has given us new priorities by which to live.

But it is pure gift on his part.

We are free to accept it or not.

Originally he made us like himself so we would be able to relate to him personally.

We can talk and hear his voice.

We do need to get our tuning right at first, for there can be static interference from our minds which can be full of so much input from our life experience.

It is our hearts that actually hear God best, and often we pay too little attention to our hearts.

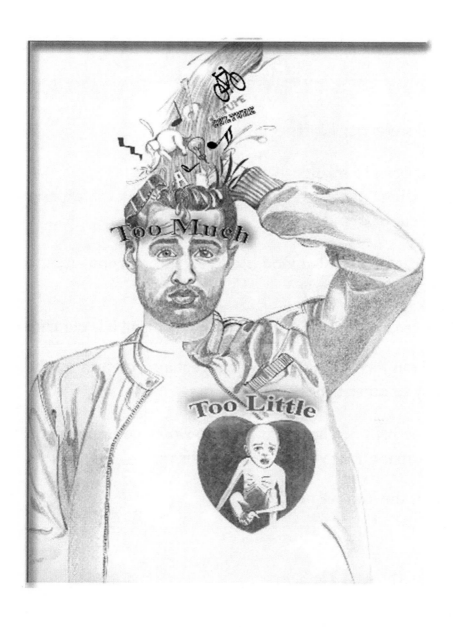

God seeks our hearts –

he is open to relationship with us.
We cannot understand this with our heads but can experience it in our hearts.

We can accept what God is offering us or pay no attention and go our own way.

We can live our lives with him or without him! It is our choice!

We can thrill his heart by our acceptance, or turn our heart away to other things.

Or perhaps our heart has been so wounded by people that we cannot trust yet that God's gift is real.

He is the love we need.

We can thank him for all the wonders he has created around us,

or

we can take it for granted and never give him a thought, too busy to notice!

If you were God, how would you feel about this?

God's patience with us is something that amazes me!

He waits!

Too busy to notice our surroundings!

He will never force us to accept him. Why? Because God IS love and love never forces, it offers and waits in hope, yet it is the strongest force in the universe!

We all know we cannot force people to love us.
We know too, that we can offer our love, yet be pushed aside and rejected which can make us wary of trying again.

God's hands are always open to us and his offer of love is always available to us.

He will never reject us!

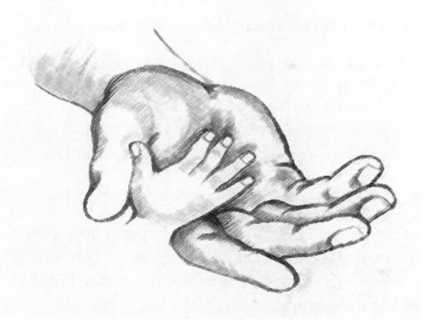

He has so much to give us, so many delights and opportunities to open for us.
He wants a warm relationship with each of us.

Do we dare to trust him?

We are here on earth to make up our minds.

God knows what we choose by the way we live.

Expectantly he watches and waits for our attention. He understands very well our reluctance and confusion, surrounded as we are by so many other alternatives.

But he hopes!

We can be stuck in rigid unbelief, refusing to budge. Then we may easily be misled into thinking we are here to enjoy ourselves – to eat, drink and be merry and then just die. This is a deception!

We are created for far more than this.

Trusting God to show us what life is all about is the first step into the MORE he is offering us.

God is calling us each by name to him.

He made us because he wants us to enjoy him forever.

We are here to choose!

Do we want him or not?

We will have what we choose!

FOREVER!

Wow!

That's quite a thought !

IT

IS

OUR

CHOICE

So what is God waiting for?

Firstly, our attention.

Secondly, our acceptance of the new way of living

he offers us, which includes:

New identity

New reason for being

New family

New purpose

   and a

New future.

A new way forward has opened for us.

Looking at what God is offering!

You may be saying:

"Wait a minute, not so fast, that sounds like a total transformation of the way I am living. Actually, I am pretty comfortable with my life as it is, so why change?"

How have you got to where you are right now? Surely there have been major changes in your life which enabled you to grow to who you see yourself to be now? I mean changes like different schools, leaving home or moving house. How about the change of sharing your life with someone, friendship, marriage, having children, doing different jobs?

We change a lot.

Actually, we are all changing all the time: each day brings the need to adapt. After all, even when we buy a new car we have to change our way of seeing the dashboard!

Living God's way involves change too. However, he will do this with us once we have agreed.

How about we throw caution to the wind and at least learn about what God is offering?

After all, it is our choice to accept or not!

Throwing caution to the wind.

Go for it !

So let's take a look at two graphics.

The first illustrates how we have come to be the person we are, in our own eyes.

Our culture has shown us our gender role and our family has trained us how to behave.

We have all learned in this way, haven't we? This is how we have come to believe who we are.

The second graphic depicts the new way God is offering us.

He offers us a new identity.

As members of his family God gives us a vision of how we can fulfill our destiny and be who he created us to be.

He will teach us how to fulfill this destiny as we live our life by his values.

We all look very carefully at bargains before we buy them to see whether they really are bargains or if there is a snag somewhere!

So, let us look more closely at all this, shall we? After all, it could be the greatest bargain of all time.

A new identity, what does this mean?

All of us have taken our identity from those who brought us up.

They gave us patterns of behaviour to follow and they showed us how to live in the culture and family into which we were born.

What did you learn as a child? What kind of experiences formed your way of thinking?

Every culture and family is different and has differing values and ways to behave, different understandings of right and wrong.

Each of us grew and absorbed these patterns of behaviour so as to fit in with the people around us. These early foundations are very deep in us. The ways we react to situations often come from patterns we learned as a child.

God wants to heal us of any wrong understandings we inherited, restore and rebuild us, and give us healthy reactions that open us to his possibilities for us.

Often our perceptions of ourselves or other people are based on our previous experience. Sometimes these can lead us into judgment and prejudice, instead of widening our understanding.

God asks us to love ourselves, but WHICH self does he mean? The one he created or the one I see myself to be?

Believing ourselves to be as God sees us is very important to our becoming that person.

As we think, so we become.

It makes sense, doesn't it, that to live God's way we need to see life through his eyes.

He invites us into his culture, or kingdom, and into his family, with his values as the guideline for our behaviour. Thus, seeing through God's eyes changes our perception of life.

Using his glasses changes our vision and our understanding. We gradually begin to appreciate God's culture, and find it working in our lives.

It is a slow process to see our former concepts of right and wrong change, but God enables us to let go of old ways and grow into his truthful version of reality.

We begin to see in a different way. His way, not ours!

Our actions will show God what we have chosen. It is that simple.

We are being offered a whole new way to see life.

Jesus called it 'being born again'!

When we join God in his culture, he joins us and enables us to live and react differently.

We learn we are valuable, unique and very special to our heavenly parent, God. As God values me, I can begin to value and love myself!

As kingdom members, we are forgiven for past errors and enter into relationship with God himself. We have a free, direct line to him at all times.

We need never live in fear and self protection ever again for God is our protector and guide and will always be there for us.

There are no circumstances he cannot turn around. He delights to show us this.

For example, whenever fear mounts in us, know he is with you, standing beside you. Then you can dismiss fear and conquer it emphatically and positively by bringing God into the situation. In other words, you are not alone. It works.

God gives us his love to assure us we can stand against anything.

He empowers us with his presence to resist fear.

So, we can cancel all fearful thoughts from our minds and declare his love and power over each situation. We can be bold and confident and fear will diminish and evaporate.

His love is stronger than fear, so which will we choose to partner with?

God loves me and will never abandon me.

He will carry me through difficult times, as I trust totally in his goodness.

He will never let me down. People may, but God never will!

God gives me security amidst life's ups and downs, through thick and thin and shows me that life with him is exciting and fulfilling.

He shows me that, with him, I can make a real difference in this world, far greater in fact than I can even imagine.

As a member of his kingdom, all this becomes possible.

I can choose to live in this reality or not.

We have a new reason for being.

God is opening up for us the reason why he created us, which is to know him, to love him, and to work together with him to bring the wonders of God to our lives on earth.

He calls us to change direction and motivation, from self-satisfaction (*I'm alright, Jack*) to coming alongside him in his great plan to destroy all evil in our world (*Mission Possible*). He will show us how!!

Self-centeredness then begins to yield to God-centeredness, and we begin to live in a new way, a way that works!

It brings us peace, joy, confidence, blessing and deep contentment as we live in this way. Our faith in his love grows and without realizing it, we do spread it around us.

It is infectious!

A new family – God's kingdom family

Whereas we originally belonged just to our natural family, we now realize that actually we can belong to his family which includes people from all nations, cultures, both genders, and is universal. We can have brothers and sisters everywhere because we can all belong to God, our heavenly parent.

Our horizons expand and we can feel a new sense of security and worth. We are part of a greater whole. We see people in a different way. We belong together. His love binds us together.

We are part of his great worldwide family. We can beam his love around the world and pray his blessing to everyone. God then showers down solutions into difficult situations.

We can make a big difference in this way.

God and we work together in partnership and we can do this from anywhere, a hospital bed, an office desk, as we rock a child to sleep or rest in our arm-chair.

We can spread his light, life, laughter and love wherever we are.

Our prayers are valuable to God and to others.

A new purpose

We all need a vision, a sense of direction, a reason to exist.

God offers us this as he calls us into unity together with him. He trains us to love like he does. This love triumphs over all difficulties. It turns all problems into opportunities to see God work.

His vision becomes ours and we increasingly long to see his love spread all over this world.

God's vision will happen! Now he invites us to bring it about with him. What an opportunity!

Our life can be really significant!

He will gently show us that our old self-oriented way of living doesn't fulfill us or bring us lasting joy. Time and time again, we learn that the old way of living just doesn't make us happy. He invites us to give up our selfishness, where everything revolves around us, because his way of love is so much better.

It builds us, encourages us and centres our focus to him.

Beauty can chase ugliness away.

Light dismisses darkness.

Hope banishes depression and a deep happiness can pervade our whole being. We begin to taste the abundant life God wants us to have.

Don't we all know of people who have spent their entire lives climbing ladders to fame, importance, or fortune only to arrive at disillusionment and loneliness?

So, having the right vision gives us the right direction and motivation and that is just what God wants to give us.

You will never be lonely with God.

Stairs going nowhere

A new future

God is inviting us to spend eternity with him.

Where do we want to end up? Eternity with him or not?

Our time here in this life is given to us to choose what we want. If we choose God we are saying to him that we want to live with him forever.

He is offering us this as our destiny.

We are spirits that live here for a time in our bodies. We have each been given free will. God waits to see if we will choose him or not.

There will be no reluctant people in heaven, only very happy ones!

All who choose him live in his kingdom both here and for eternity.

Wow! An eternity of happiness and purpose!

None of us knows what heaven is like, even if we have had glimpses of it, but we do know it will be a place of love and wonder greater than we can even imagine. He is inviting us to share this with him!

He sent Jesus to show us the way.

He knew we would not believe all this unless we could see a living human example of how all this can be real.

Jesus said, "Love God with all of your being and each other as you love yourself." Then He showed us how, by living this way.

You may have seen this picture of Jesus a million times, but hopefully now it means a little more to you.

Divine love is not the same as our human love.

So what does this divine love look like?

This love never gives up. It keeps on going.

It cares for others unselfishly and does not put self first.

Love does not strut, seeking a stage.

Love is patient, it knows how to wait.

It does not fly off the handle, and is not easily offended or provoked.

Love does not keep a score of the faults of others, nor talk about them to others.

Love does not gossip.

It does not revel when others are down, nor delight to take advantage.

Love always looks for the best and does not entertain negative thinking.

Love does not look back but keeps moving forward with its eyes on the goal.

We cannot love like this ourselves on a consistent basis. We know that – it is pretty hard and we are human! But with God we CAN learn to love this way!

God wants to empower us to do so by walking every step of life with us. Together with him all things are possible.

He wants us to experience his love ourselves and then, together with him, take it to the whole world.

Are you saying that we can rise above our natural limitations and live our lives with him?

Yes, and as we do, we spread his love all over this world. We can't help it, for it flows out of us.

Nothing evil can withstand his love. Evil flees in the face of true love! Real love conquers fear.

Many people have proved this by standing strong in the face of adversity. William Wilberforce stood against slavery. It looked an impossible task at first, everyone in power was against him. Yet he persevered, and he saw slavery stopped. Just one man made such a difference.

We have all been chosen by God to make a stand, each in our own lives. God will show us how and empower us to do it. We have a unique destiny to fulfill that can only be done in union with God. It is never too late to start, for with God it is possible.

Let us not settle for less!

What a **challenge!**

What an **incentive!**

What a **destiny!**

What an **adventure!**

When it finally dawned on me that this is what life is about, I remember saying to God, "But I don't know how to love!"

He just said to me, quietly in my heart, "**Come to me and I will show you. I am offering you abundant life, and as you come close to me you will learn how to live my way. Come!**"

I did, and I am proving this to be true every day in my life.

So, I don't want you to miss out on all that God is offering just because no-one has ever told you.

The only way you will ever prove this to be true for yourself is to ask God to show you in his unique way.

He said, "**Ask and you will receive. Knock and the door will be opened.**"

Why not ask?

Talk to God and tell him you want to get to know him better. Get serious about seeking him and ignore everything that could block your determination.

Get focused!

He has said, "If you seek me, you will find me." So, start a definite search.

God is love. He made you so he could share himself with you in an ever-deepening relationship of trust.

Anything that increases this relationship, go for it! Don't leave God out in the cold. Take him into your day. Talk to him, heart to heart, and follow his lead.

Enjoy the adventure!

Your choice!

Having read Chapters 1 and 2, please select your next choice.

If you want to see how other people found God.
Then read Chapter 3.

You may want to know more about the person Jesus, that God sent. Chapter 4 will introduce you to him.

Perhaps you are interested to know how the author learned all this, then please join me in Chapter 5.

Happy reading!

CHAPTER THREE

People's Real Stories

Drawings created by our grandchildren

We have seen that God is love and that he wants us to receive this love and spread it to the whole world.

Each day can be an exciting walk with him as we learn how to love his way.

"Good morning, God, what shall we do together today?"

I LIKE ME
GOD LIKES ME!

Chapter three is full of stories written from people's own experience of how they got to know God is real.

I will never forget the man whom I was nursing in hospital. He had had a massive heart attack and was on totally flat bed rest, unable to do anything for himself.

While I was attending to his needs, he said, "This is the best thing that has happened to me in years!"

I was in my early twenties and that got my attention! Lying flat, unable to do anything, how could that be the best thing? This is what he said:

TOM THE BAKER'S STORY

'God gives me a future and a hope.' Jeremiah.29:11

"You see, I am a baker, and I'm good at what I do. I started with one shop, now I have five, and every night I do what I like most, I bake! I thought I had got life sussed. I mean, I have a lovely family, a great couple of kids, I love my wife and we easily meet the bills. Then suddenly out of the blue, I am flat on my back in hospital. The only thing I can do is think! So I have been wondering, what is this life all about? Why am I here on earth. There must be a reason why I am here; what is it? Am I fulfilling it? I mean, I know God made me, but am I doing what He created me for or just enjoying myself? I could miss the reason why He created me!

That's why I am saying this is the best thing that has happened to me, because for the first time in years I am talking to God about all this. If I go out of this hospital my life will change."

He did leave and I am sure he kept his word.

I bless him because I never forgot what he told me.

Let me introduce to you Christine who is a lovely young woman. These are her words:

CHRISTINE'S STORY

'God heals the broken-hearted.' Luke 4:18

"About three months ago I attempted suicide for the third time. After a dark struggle for ten years with various psychological disorders, I had finally had enough. This time I came closer to death than any of the others. This suicide attempt left me with serious physical injuries. I was angry and sad and was in a lot of pain physically, and in intense emotional and mental pain. I was in the same dark hopeless place I was in before, nothing had changed. I've been a Christian all my life and despite all the Christian books, seminars, Bible studies and Church ministries I was a part of, I felt suffocated by darkness and despair that was endless. I was desperate for freedom but I could not find it. I took your Resurrected Life class* about a month after my suicide attempt. The first few classes I attended, I was in so much physical pain as I was still recovering, so I did not even hear most of what was said, but I somehow knew it was important to be there anyway.

One night, during the ministry, I saw a young man accept God into his life for the first time. I watched as God transformed this man's life in that single hour. I've seen people come to God but this time it had an impact on me like never before. It was like God had prepared my heart for this moment. God had brought me to a place in my life where I was desperately searching and properly listening. Watching the process as this man was saved, left me speechless and in awe. I saw with my heart God's amazing love. I had seen a miracle and it totally changed my life. Slowly my eyes were opened to the truth of God's love, mercy and freedom. This was the freedom I had been searching for. I felt Him slowly untie the ropes of misery that held me back. I began to breathe and finally feel what freedom really was. I had been a prisoner for over ten years and had just been set free. I had thought this was impossible but I now know that nothing is impossible with God. He is a God of freedom-from-darkness, release from misery and depression. He is the living light. He has set me free and for the first time in my life, I have joy."

Christine continued in her new-found freedom!

Christine

God calls us all, but often we do not hear him.

We can be brought up in a church but have never really met God. We can go to church every Sunday but still never know the wonder of God's love. We have just learned to go through the motions, so to speak; not really experiencing anything life-changing. Everyone's experience is so different. God's way with each is unique, that is because we are so special to him.

TIM'S STORY

'God is my refuge and strength, a present help in times of trouble.' Psalm. 46:1

Tim met God in prison. He said,

"The first time I knew God was real was when I was locked up doing time. God touched my heart and showed me that I was his child. He protected me in those bad times in prison and gave me strength to believe in his love. Now I have a son and I know he is a gift of God to me."

RICHARD'S STORY

'I will be his Father and he will be my son.' 2 Samuel 7:14

Richard expressed it this way. "I was raised by a single mother, but now I realize that I do have a father. With God as my Father, I am strong and able to overcome the alcohol and lust addictions that I have struggled with most of my life."

CAROL'S STORY

'He will guide them to springs of life-giving water.'
Revelation 7:17

"After coming to the Lord, I was able to leave behind me a life of witchcraft, drug addiction and confused sexuality. Depression ran through both sides of my family.

But now, through God's grace, I have seen this broken not only in me but also some of my family."

BRIAN'S STORY

'There is no fear in love for perfect love casts out all fear.'
I John 4:18

Brian told me,

"I was twelve years old, when God talked to me. It was in my bedroom that I heard him talk to me. He said, "I love you and I will never leave you. Your earthly parents do not know how to love and take care of you, but I will be there for you all the time. All the hard times and the good times I will be there for you. Remember, I love you." Through my whole life I had never heard the words "I love you," so when Father God told me that, I knew he was talking to me."

ANN'S STORY

'So they went out and preached that people should turn away from their sins and they cast out many demons.' Mark 6:12

"I had been a Christian over twenty five years, taught Bible studies and led a quiet "Christian life", though I was not totally positive that God was there. I usually thought He was, but to be honest, I would have my doubt times. It wasn't until about four years ago in the middle of the night that I experienced something that made me realize that I know that I know God exists. I had never been face to face with demons until four years ago. I acknowledged that hell and satan existed, because the Bible spoke of them, but I didn't really think much about satan's power because I had never seen that power. I certainly didn't think his demons had the ability to get into my "Christian family" who went to church.

We were awakened into the spiritual realm when one of our sons became demonised and my husband and I did not know what to do. Our quiet Christian life never taught us anything about that. Through a series of events my son was ministered to by a godly friend over a course of time, but it was obvious that there was still a controlling demon holding on to him.

On that particular night, my son was very tormented at home, and it was apparent we could not control what was going on by ourselves at our house. I called a friend and she told me to bring him to her house because she knew the time had come. When we arrived it was about midnight, and my son was beyond what I could deal with in my safe little life. Something truly evil was manifesting, I was terrified to say the least. That wild person was my son who I had given birth to and had loved and raised - what had happened to him? I was amazed how God worked through our friend. She had such strength, confidence and authority as she used God's power to rid my son of the horrible evil. However, she was such a sweet little woman in her own personality.

It was clearly not something that a person could do alone. Witnessing my son's deliverance was proof that God REALLY EXISTS, plain and simple."

JOHN'S STORY

'Whoever does not receive the Kingdom of God like a child will never enter it.' Luke 18:17

John, now in his forties, said,

"I was eight years old when I first really knew that God was real. I knew about God from Sunday school but I knew he was real when He answered my prayer. I went to a school where the boys made fun of any boy who went to sit on the toilet. They would come in and make rude fun and I hated it. So, I remember saying to God, "Look, if when I have to go to the toilet I sing songs I learned in Sunday school to you, do you think you could keep the boys out for me?" No boy ever bothered me again in this way."

That was the start of John's trust in God.

CHARLES' STORY

'Let the children come to Me and do not stop them because
the Kingdom of God belongs to such as these.'
Luke 18:16

"When I was a little boy my mother told me that she could
not stand me, that nobody loved me and everyone hated
me. She said they were only nice to me because they felt
sorry for me. I went away crying and she added how stupid I
was and that she wished me dead!

But when I was crying and scared, God told me that
He loved me. I felt Him hug me and I fell asleep. I always
remember that voice deep in my heart."

JASON'S STORY

'At night when people are asleep God speaks in dreams and visions.' Job 33:15

Jason said, "The way I was living would be considered sinful. I did drugs and drinking. 95% of the people I hung around with did not know God. One day I got fed-up with everything. That was the first time I thought about ending my life. That night I had a dream:

I was standing next to a cliff edge at night overlooking the city lights and then I looked up and saw something coming towards me. It looked like Jesus. He took my hand. I knew everything that he was thinking. I felt God's love. Then he flew away. I don't remember asking God for help that night but that was when I knew God was real."

SONIA'S STORY

'Know the truth and the truth shall make you free.'
John 8:32'

"You know, now I realize I have always looked down on myself as a child and felt ashamed, but now I see that that is not how God made me, nor how he sees me, so why should I? I have given him all these negative feelings I felt about myself and instead accepted his version of me as the truth. Now I feel happy about myself from the inside-out."

Before   After

PAUL'S STORY

'It is impossible to please God without faith, since anyone
who comes to Him must believe He exists and rewards
those who try to find Him.' Hebrews 11:6

I've always believed that God existed but, for half my life, He was not real to me. This was despite being confirmed into the Church of England and praying many times after receiving Communion that He would touch me in some real, tangible way.

I had trained and qualified as an accountant. The business world was my oyster; I could do anything! It took a disaster in a job to make me realize that I had taken a step too far in my career and that outside events were more in control of my life than I was.

At that point, my sister Jean, a strong, committed Christian, stepped into my life in a new way, but me being the 'professional accountant' I am, I would only rely on concrete facts and experiences, never just on faith.

One of the major stumbling blocks for me was the apparent variety of Christian faiths. They weren't all the same, so which was the right one? At this point, Jean gave up. I had exhausted her library of answers, so she wheeled in the curate from her church. He patiently went through all my questions again until we came to the $64,000 one.
"If I am to become a Christian, won't I have to join the church Jesus founded (meaning the Roman Catholic Church)?" His reply floored me. "If that's what it takes to make you choose to be a Christian, go ahead and join the RC church."
You have to know that my family was Anglican, and uncompromisingly anti-Catholic. Yet here was an Anglican priest pointing me in the direction of the RCs. My final intellectual objection was blown to smithereens. That night, Jean gave me Norman Warren's little booklet 'Journey Into Life' and told me to go to bed and read it quietly on my own. In a dozen or so pages Norman explains Christianity in a very simple way. You can't misunderstand his message. By now, I was close, but not there yet!

Back in my days of taking Communion I had asked God to become real in my life, and as I saw it, He hadn't. Norman's explanations all fitted the story I well knew, so now it was up to God to supply the last piece of the jigsaw. I put the booklet down and said into thin air, "God, if you are real, prove it to me." Instantly I was surrounded by this sense and feeling of being wrapped in warm cotton-wool. He had cocooned me in his arms. The feeling stayed with me for three days, and I walked on air. Then the reality of who I am and my previous, boring church experiences stepped back in. I refused to agree that something special had happened . . . it had been a short-term experience, so wouldn't last and wouldn't impact my life.

We attended a service at a church recommended to us back home, and it was the usual, dreary, uninspiring ritual . . . until we came to sharing the Peace (greeting those around me peacefully). This was brand new to me as a church experience. Suddenly everything Jesus said came to life; church came to life; and I came to life.

It had taken me about three weeks from my encounter with God to allowing myself to accept that something had really happened. I had been aware that during those days God had been behind me, following me around, waiting patiently for the penny to drop and then graciously giving me the final proof my mind needed.

Knowing He was real made me hungry for Him. In the mid '70s, the charismatic renewal was all the rage, so I quickly got to know about the Holy Spirit . . . but Jesus. I had no inner confirmation of who or what he was. Again God graciously stepped in and gave me this in a way I could understand.

I have spent the intervening years trying to come to grips with why I am here, what the job is that He built me to do, and (falteringly) trying to do it. Despite all the times I trip up and fall flat on my face, having to get up and brush myself down, He is still there, lifting me up and urging me to take the next step.

This God loves me. This God is in me. This God accepts me for who I am. This God wants the best for me, and daily is changing me into the son He first thought me to be. This God is my God for eternity.

NEGATIVENESS

HOPE

God is real and each person's story is unique because we are special to **him.**

Whether we feel special or not, this is the truth. (God says so!)

How will we answer his invitation?

Our lives will show him our answer!

To miss God is the greatest calamity that could happen to us.

The ball is in our court.

Am I talking 'religion?' NO

Am I talking relationship? YES

with

- The God who holds the universe in his hands.

- The God who LOVES us and wants us to enjoy him.

- The Designer of a baby's smile.

- The One who gives peace and contentment to the aged.

- The Artist who paints each sunset and warms each human heart.

- The Creator of abundant joy who sings us into being.

- The One who never turns away from us.

- The One who can heal every wound and delight your heart.

God is calling your name.

Do answer him.

Your next choice, should you continue to read, is:

Chapter 4 which tells you more about Jesus' life and message,

and

Chapter 5 which tells you more about the author.

Enjoy your read!

CHAPTER FOUR

The one God sent

Getting to Know You

If you have chosen this chapter, then you want to know more about the person called Jesus, whom God sent to show us how to live as God designed us to live.

He lived an exemplary life. He gave us a model to follow in the ups and downs of life that worked then and works now.

He showed us so much about who God actually is, and how possible it is to live life God's way. Actually, Jesus represented God perfectly as man. If we want to know about God, then we should study Jesus' life for He lived in union with God all the time.

So, let's look at his life together, shall we?

Jesus was born in Bethlehem and the unique happenings surrounding his birth have been carefully chronicled for us to read in the four Gospels of Matthew, Mark, Luke and John in the New Testament part of the Bible.

He grew up in Nazareth and lived just like any other Jewish boy at that time. He worked as a carpenter there until he was thirty years old. His cousin John was called by God to alert people that the one God had promised to show them how to live was already among them.

John was well known as he tried to get people to focus on what God was doing. One day he pointed to Jesus as the one God had promised, and God confirmed this by declaring from heaven in a clear, audible voice that Jesus was His son in whom he was well pleased.

Many people witnessed this and went away wondering what it could mean. You see, they knew that in their Jewish history God had promised to send someone who would change their lives forever. God does not make promises he does not keep, and they knew this to be true for God had saved them from their enemies throughout many centuries.

So, the question in the minds of those who heard this voice from heaven that day was, "What does this mean?" Was it God's answer to their present problems (occupation by the Roman overlords), or was this the time when God would deliver them from the greater evil that oppressed their lives? What did this voice mean by "This is my son?"

So it was understandable that a few young men, Andrew, Peter, James and John followed Jesus to find out where he lived and who he was. Jesus invited them to stay with him, and this they and several others did for three years. They became eyewitnesses to how Jesus lived, what he did for people and what he taught. (Much later they wrote it all down so future generations could know the wonder of all this. You and I can read it in the Gospels in the Bible.)

They heard Jesus refer to God as his Father. This was new to them, but they remembered that God had declared him to be his son. They wondered what all this could mean. They watched what he did and knew no-one had ever done what he was doing. So, who was he?

That is an all-important question. He proved who he was by the way he lived, and people watched and were filled with wonder.

One day they met a funeral procession on the road—a single mum was walking behind the coffin of her only son, weeping. Jesus touched the coffin and the young man was restored to life. Imagine how his mother felt! It caused quite a stir.

Another day, while walking along, he saw a group of lepers ringing their bells, telling people to keep away. Jesus went up to them and told them they were healed. All ten were healed that day. Can you imagine what that did for them? No-one had done that before, so who was this guy? Word spread like wildfire and people flocked to Jesus to be healed, bringing their loved ones on stretchers long distances, and everyone who came was healed.

One day Jesus and his friends went to a lonely place to get some rest, but thousands followed them. So Jesus fed them all by multiplying a child's packed lunch! They all ate their fill and there was plenty left over.

No wonder they followed him! And as they came he taught them of the ways God wanted them to live. He taught them to bless and not curse, to forgive others, not to retaliate; to value others, not to look down on them; to give mercy and compassion, not judgment and revenge. He taught them how to love and demonstrated it through his kindness and ability to help them.

Quickly he became the topic on everyone's lips. Could this guy be the one they had been longing for, for so long? Simple people flocked to him, children felt safe with him, but there were those who were jealous and this grew into hatred. Their hearts were blocked to his goodness and they spread lies and rumours, even calling him evil.

Jesus tried to reach them but their hearts were set against him, and finally they trapped him and turned the crowd against him. How did Jesus respond? Always in love, and this was his greatest demonstration of God's love. He allowed them to kill him publically (in those days this entailed crucifixion) and although he could have saved himself, he chose not to, to prove that love does not retaliate but forgives even at this level. He lived what he had been preaching, even to loving those who were crucifying him, because he knew they did not know who he was or understand what they were doing. In the natural we cannot love to that degree, but Jesus showed us that is how God loves.

Jesus showed that we can now come close to God without fear for God will forgive us as Jesus forgave those who killed him. It is as though Jesus became a bridge by which all of us can come to God and know he will forgive and welcome us. God chose this wonderful way to show us the depth of this truth.

Jesus had said, "Greater love has no man than he lay down his life for his friends." Then he did just that so we could become God's friends. If we choose friendship with God we will be his friends forever—heaven is a reality!

God raised Jesus from death to life and he was seen by many people who then really believed what he had told them. He trained his disciples and told them to go to all people and show them how to live just as he had demonstrated. He told them that he would be with them always and they could count on him.

What had started from one man quickly spread: this whole idea of living in love, not fear; living in tune with God, not our deeply selfish ways; blessing, not grumbling and cursing; forgiving, not retaliating; thinking thoughts of love, not fear. Jesus showed us how it could be done. He calls us to him even now, and empowers us to live as he did. As we do, he gives us his Spirit and we will see the sick healed and the oppressed set free, just as he did. This is happening in many places in today's world.

As we choose to live as God designed us to do here, so God offers us to live with him forever. This is the invitation God is offering us all. He waits to see if we will accept. He hopes we will. But it is our choice! This is the message Jesus asked us to give to the world. It has been proclaimed through the ages. It is what is called the Good News.

In the seventeen hundreds, Charles Wesley summed it up in the Christmas song we all know but may not have really pondered.

Hark! the herald angels sing,
Glory to the newborn King.
Peace on earth and mercy mild,
God and sinners reconciled.
Joyful all ye nations rise.

Join the triumph of the skies;
With the angelic host proclaim,
Christ is born in Bethlehem!

Christ by highest heaven adored,
Christ the everlasting Lord.
Late in time, behold him come,
Offspring of the Virgin's womb.
Veiled in flesh the Godhead see,
Hail, the incarnate deity.
Pleased as man with man to dwell,
Jesus our Immanuel. *(God with us).*

Hail the heaven-born prince of peace,
Hail the son of righteousness.
Light and life to all he brings,
Risen with healing in his wings.
Mild he lays his glory by,
Born that man no more may die.
Born to raise the sons of earth,
Born to give them second birth.

Hark, the herald angels sing,
glory to the newborn King.

It's always good to read things for ourselves, so why not read Mark's Gospel which tells us how Jesus lived and what he taught. Jesus singled Peter out. Mark was Peter's secretary and wrote down Peter's first hand eyewitness experience, as he had lived with Jesus constantly for the last three years of his life. Peter finally gave his life rather than deny that this was the truth.

As you read, ask God to reveal the truth to you. It could change your life.

As I write, one thing occurs to me: Jesus only healed those who came to him. People would tell people about him, but then it was up to those who heard to go and meet him so they would see for themselves and believe. They often travelled far at great inconvenience; it is much easier for us. All we need to do is talk to God sincerely and open our hearts to listen to him.

This is the first step. We cannot take the second step until we take the first. That is how we all learned to walk! It is the same here.

OK! If I should choose this way, how do I start?

Firstly, open your mind, really open it. Leave all doubts and disbelief aside and talk to God as a real person. He is right there with you! He wants you to talk to him. Start this relationship and build it in every way you can. He will show you how! Relationships always take time to build, but you will be amazed how it happens. Start living with him in your daily life.

Secondly, as his presence becomes more and more real to us, we start doing what he has designed us to do. As we become free in his love so we see that love flows out to others as it did in Jesus' life. People get healed, lives change as his power demolishes the hang-ups that have stopped them living full and happy lives.

Thirdly, God's plan becomes our focus too and we begin to see reality through his eyes.—Life makes more sense, it even becomes exciting. Millions worldwide are currently opting for God's solution to life down here. We do not hear that on the TV news (why not, you may ask?) but be assured it is happening. God is building a community of power that will change this world from darkness to light, from fear to love. Do we want to join him in this?

It can only happen as we each individually choose it to. The invitation is real. Which way will we choose to live, our way or the way God offers? The life we have always lived or the abundant life God makes possible? Do we continue to accept that life will always be like it is now, or will we take the challenge that our life could really make a difference in this world?

Opportunity knocks, why not talk to God about it?

C. S. Lewis is reported to have said that Jesus was one of three things:

A great liar, insane, or he was who he said he was: the Son of God!

Why not read for yourself and find out?

The New Testament—God's story

CHAPTER FIVE

My story of how all this became real for me

Looking out of my tiny bedroom window at the beauty of the night sky, I found myself saying aloud, "Whoever made you (the moon) must be very beautiful." Immediately in my inner self I knew that the one who had made the moon had also made me, and that somehow I was special to him, for a warm loving presence filled my room. That night God became my Father, and I was no longer lonely, nor was I afraid, for I knew He was there looking after me and He was all powerful. He would protect me, even as later the bombs fell. So I would talk to him at times. That is when my relationship with God started. I was eight years old.

I was born in India to British parents in 1927. My father knew me for only two months because he dropped dead of a massive heart attack. This circumstance altered my life. We left India and returned to Britain.

I soon realized that most children had both father and mother, so why didn't I have a dad? There was a bond between my brother and my mother and I knew there would have been that bond between my dad and me, but why, I wondered wasn't he there? For the first eight years of my life I wondered and longed for what I did not have. I never expressed this but it tugged at my heart as an unanswered question. Now I see the reason why it had to happen that way. I see that had Dad lived I would have developed into quite a different person. Things happen to us that cause us to think of life, and of our role in it in certain ways. We react to daily circumstances and this conditions us to see ourselves in a certain light. But are we really this person? The answer to this question is NO!

So who am I? It has taken me many years to find the answer to this question. I am learning still, because I have found that I am not defined by what my parents gave me genetically. Present-day science tells us that our genetic code is not carved in stone. Actually, our thoughts are capable of changing our genetic code. (For confirmation, read Dr. Caroline Leaf's book "Who switched off my brain?").

It also dawned on me that I am not what the circumstances of my early life conditioned me to become. I am not the result of all that has happened to me in my life. I realized that accepting this view would dwarf my full potential and true identity.

So who am I? I now know that I am a creation of a loving God, the God I first met as I gazed at the beauty of the moon. What I didn't know then was that he had created me for a purpose, and that I am being offered a future and a destiny in his great plan if I choose his way of living this life. So how did I learn that? Let me share this with you.

I once believed a pretty damaged version of myself because I took in as truth the negative judgments people made about who they thought I was. I found myself unable to compete with my brother for my mother's affection and thought that, compared to the rest of my family, I was below expectation. I apologised a lot and threw myself into sport as the one thing I was good at. But God was always there for me and at seventeen someone shared with me who Jesus was. I learned that God loved us all so much that Jesus came to earth to show us what God's love looked like. This became real to me. I realized he had given his life to remove the barriers between people and God. This meant that I could know his love for ME and enter into it. I fell in love with Jesus that day. I was seventeen.

I thought that as he had given his life for me, I could do nothing better but give my life to him. I did not know what that meant, but I put my life into God's hands to do with as he wanted.

I began to realize that if God loved me, then I must be of value. Obviously, what God thinks is truth! Therefore, to see myself in any other way would be to disagree with God. I had learned that it is counter-productive to disagree with God, no matter how right it may seem to other people or to me. God's way of seeing had to be the right one, so perhaps I was not the sub-standard person I saw myself to be. I began to replace my negativity with what God says about all of us.

"I love you with an everlasting love," "God washes me clean and gives me a new heart," "God created me in his image" and "He joys over me with singing."

I was learning that each one of us is extremely important to God or he would not have created us. I have learned that God hates the hurtful negative things in life that have tried hard to distort our concept of him. His truth opposes the lies we have taken in and believed, which have given us a wrong version of life and of who we are created to be. God heals these distortions as we bring them to him and agree to give up our negative reactions of hatred, resentment and disappointment. Then we can move on into the life he intends for us.

So I started to deliberately let go of the negative hurtful happenings, and other people's estimations of me. I did this by chucking negativity out of my mind and focusing instead on how marvellous God is and His love for me. The truth is that 'nothing can separate me from his love.'

As I did this, to my amazement, I started to react differently. God was changing me! I became lighter and brighter and much happier as a result!

If God is love, I thought, then the name of the game is Love, pure and simple. It is not theology, nor great revelations that satisfy our minds and consume much of our time but have little effect on how we live life. It is simply a question of love: how much love is there in our life? What kind of love is there in our life? Do we love at all? Because if we don't have love, we do not know God at all, for he is love.

It was with this ringing in my soul that I approached God. "Lord, I do not know how to love. Please teach me," I said.

I began to realize that all my life God had been teaching me about love through all sorts of people and circumstances. As I looked at the various chapters of my journey in this life, I now saw that he had been there all the time, though I had not realized this. I had not been able to see it that way at the time. My confidence in his love began to grow, and as it did I began to grow into my true self. My insecurity gave way to confidence **in him.** Slowly I became rock-solid in knowing that God was always there and I could count on him even when people let me down and when my whole world turned upside down. I knew deep within me he would hold me strong and he did. I fell more and more in love with the dependability of God. I began to want to fulfill his concept of me and to look beyond myself at him.

I wonder, does this make sense to you? Can you relate to my journey?

Perhaps we all start life with the wrong glasses. We view everything from our own perspective of how it affects us. We are essentially self-centred, everything revolves around me, the mighty Me. How I think; how I understand; how I feel; how things affect Me; how people act towards Me. It's always Me at the centre of my life. We all start that way and we can remain that way all of our life, can't we?

If we do, we will miss what God is offering us, because love is the opposite of self-centredness. This realization brought me up sharp.

We have all met people who remain centred on themselves. They are hard to please, demand much of others; they are usually prickly for they will not let others come close; they are not happy people. Naturally we steer clear and protect ourselves from their negativity. Yet, if we are honest we do recognize that these tendencies are deep in all of us. We can all be touchy and downright awkward at times. Even as we try to change, we can easily fall back into selfish ways, get depressed and even fed up with ourselves. The painful truth slowly dawns on us that we cannot truly change the selfishness of our hearts ourselves. It is too deeply ingrained. Only God can do that.

As we grow closer to God, he gives us his love, the Holy Spirit who transforms our hard heart and enables us to love his way.

God breathes new life into us, and this sets us free from old habits, old ways of seeing, and fills us with light, life, laughter and love. I know this to be true because I see it happen all the time. He is transforming me from the inside out. It is exciting. I am not the person I used to be.

The good news I have learned is that, as I set my focus off myself and onto God and learn to trust him, my life will change. It did and it does! It is a process and it requires our co-operation.

I had begun by looking around me at what God had created. There is so much beauty to see, so much loveliness that I can focus on, if I so choose. Beauty in sound, in colour, in texture, beauty that I admire in people, beauty even in me. It occurred to me that if I filled my mind with beauty I would begin to reflect this around me. After all, it is what we are full of that spills out of us. It is what is in the glass that matters, not the glass itself!

My mother had once said to me when I had answered her back angrily, "Molly, a cup that is full of love cannot spill bitterness, no matter how sharply it is knocked!" I began to watch my reactions!

This led me to look at what was coming out of me more carefully. I was appalled! So much negativity was coming from my lips. Wow! What was I spreading everywhere I went? I realized too that what came out of my mouth was first in my head; I never said anything I had not first thought. My mind needed to change. How many conversations were going on in my head? Who am I talking to? Why am I talking to them? Doesn't that take up a lot of my energies? If I stopped doing this wouldn't I be more peaceful? So I started monitoring my thoughts and asked God to help me clean up my thought life. Then I found I could hear God much better.

All of us are responsible for what we are spreading around us, is it good news or bad, does it uplift or depress? God has given all of us free will, so we are responsible for how we use it. We can choose what we allow into our minds and therefore what we speak out of our mouths.

I began to play a game with my mind. "Ah! Watch it, that was not worth saying, now was it?" At first, this realization made me feel guilty. but gradually I saw that this was because I expected myself to do differently. Could that guilt be based in pride? As I saw that it was, I began to give it quietly to the Lord and ask him to replace it with his love. He did, and guilt changed to gratitude that he wanted to change me. What I could not do, he delighted in doing.

There were other things that needed changing too. I saw that fear was an enemy to be resisted at all times. For if I truly believed God was for me, why be afraid? Surely fear was the exact opposite of love and trust, and could damage my relationship with him. Fear was a "no, no," and as I dismissed its hold on me and counted on God, I grew in love and confidence in him. I began to see that I am his masterpiece in the making. As Michelangelo saw the statue of David in the block of marble and chipped away until it was completed, so God, through the circumstances of my life, was enabling his first vision of me to be recreated. I began to want to cooperate with him more fully. Thus, my whole attitude began to change. For instance, I began to look for something good about a person who was being obnoxious and comment on it, "Oh, you know you do have a lovely smile, it lights up your face," or "I do like the colour you are wearing," or whatever seemed appropriate. After all, the reason they are being difficult is that they don't know yet how not to be, so "Lord, please help them." These are simple changes in our thinking and reactions but they can become habits that help us learn how to love. They condition us to be able to receive love too.

Perhaps what helped me most in this transformation of mind and attitude was the realization that the Holy Spirit lived in me and would change me if I let him. As I have said, I knew the Father when I was 8, the Son when I was 17, but now I met the wonder of the Holy Spirit, thanks to the outpouring of grace called the Charismatic renewal. I was in my fourties.

I learned the value of walking in the light with others and not being so insular within myself. I realized that people who came to Jesus were healed by Jesus bringing their problems out into the open, like the man with the withered hand hidden under his cloak. Jesus said, "Stretch forth your hand," in front of everyone. As the man did, he was healed.

In my British culture I had been trained to hide problems and try to stiff-upper-lip them. Now I saw that was not the way Jesus taught. I found that opening myself to those who were teaching me spiritually was very difficult. But, every time I did, healing happened in me. I began to be really led by the Holy Spirit and not my own way of coping. My various masks fell off. I gave up trying to be Christian and allowed God to make me real. As this happened, I became more loving to others and more open to them loving me. A leader once told me, "Molly, you will always know a real Christian because they build people up." Very true!

God sees us as we really are. He knows the best way we need to change. He will show us our need and then empower us to change. It can be something we do together. This relationship can grow deeper and deeper, and as we count on his transformation of us, we see him at work in our lives and we begin to really know that he is for us 100%. Love grows as we see this happen. He is infinitely able to work with us.

To enable a person to come from deep self-centeredness to the wonder of divine love is God's focus. And as each one is transformed so the whole globe can be. Can you imagine a world without selfishness, where love reigns supreme? This is the future plan of God and he is inviting us to join him in making this happen. Wow! So, by loving in God's way with his Holy Spirit, together, we can change the world! I recalled a little song we used to sing as children,

"Jesus bids us shine with a clear, pure light.

Like a little candle burning in the night,

In this world of darkness, Jesus bids us shine,

You in your small corner, and me in mine."

I began to see that with God all things are possible and if we had millions of lit candles, the world would indeed change. I became on fire to see this happen and I wanted to be a part of his great plan. So, I prayed,

"Lord make me an instrument of your peace, where there is hatred let me sow love, where there is injury, your pardon Lord."

The prayer of St Francis had become special to me at that time. God heard my prayer and he trained me to see people as he did, not with my natural mind but to look deeper to find the person he had created them to be. Then I could accept them warts and all, just as He accepts me. My natural judgment must yield if his love is to rule the day; blessing replace criticism; and prayer for their well-being replace my expectation that they be different. I began to realize there is power in the right way to pray, and I saw the difference in my own life and eventually in other people's.

People started to come to see me. They were of all ages and stages of life, but one thing they had in common was that life seemed pointless, for they were struggling with many problems. At first I thought God must have made a mistake, "Why me?" I thought, "What have I to give them?" He pulled me up sharp. "Molly, you have Me, do not say you have nothing to give. Give Me!"

I have learned that when we work with God, and allow him to minister to others, the burdens they have carried all their lives fall off their backs. The lies that have controlled them, so that they cannot fly free as God intends, can be dismissed as his truth replaces these lies. People can be set free to be who God created them to be, for 'streams of living water' can flow out from us to them, just as Jesus promised. I have no clue how this happens, all I know is that it always does. We all say after ministering, "Wow! He has done it again!"

God has thus brought to birth Resurrected Life Ministry (RLM) through me, and as people from every walk of life have come, we have seen thousands of lives changed. He called us to join him in seeing people set free, the broken-hearted healed, those blinded by this world able to see in God's way and live free in his glorious truth. RLM is a discipleship ministry which teaches and enables people to do just that. It has nothing to do with money, for God had said to me "What I have given you free, give freely." In the US it is a nonprofit organization and abides by the rules of that culture. RLM gives apprenticeship training to those who want the "Abundant Life" Jesus came to give us, and to spread it to others. It is just amazing to see this happen. (You can check our internet website if you wish, Resurrectedlife.org for how this happens.)

I was born in India and trained as a nun, nurse, teacher, head-mistress of a school; over the decades of my life I have been a wife, mother, widow, mature graduate student in a different culture, and went to further train missionaries in various countries; and now God has given me Resurrected Life Ministry to enrich people's lives. God has given me insight into many different aspects of life and perhaps he is making me a bridge to bring unity wherever I go.

Each of us has a role to play in God's great drama. This is my role and for this I was created and skillfully shaped by him through life.

God changes us and then others through us, and thus his love spreads across the world. But can we trust ourselves to him? There is so much in us that wants to protect ourselves, and we find trusting very difficult, don't we? That's why letting God free to work with us takes time. We are reluctant to let go. Yet, I learned that every time I did, I grew closer to him and wanted him more. I found silence very helpful as I learned to shut out the urgency of my mind. I found that when resting in an inner stillness I could know God far better: grasping moments with him became a necessity to my communication and dependency on him. I found that keeping my focus on what he wanted and seeing through his eyes, every happening in my life became my adventure. I saw, at last, that this life is a glorious love affair with God; it is an invitation into the wonder of his love that will last for eternity.

His patience with us, with me, is just awe-inspiring!

We really do choose the depth of relationship with God we want. God offers us all that He is. But he knows that as fragile human beings too much too soon would over-power us and make us run away, timid to try again! So he is very gentle with us as we learn. That is why it takes time! Relationship is like that, isn't it?

Think of your own relationships with people; it is hard to trust someone with your inner self, isn't it? What will they do, will they come too close too soon, will they demand too much of me? Will they misunderstand me? Will I get hurt like last time?

Be assured God never hurts, people do! God will never overwhelm us because he wants so much for us to dare to come close to him. But slowly and with infinite care he will detach us from things and people that can lead us away from him. As we move towards him he will guide and guard and enable, but only as much as we want. He is the expert at relationship, of course he is, he is God!

Life has become truly exciting. Each day is an opportunity to know God better and see his love spread to me and from me to the people around me. It has become exhilarating to be alive and to see others come to know the truth of who God sees them to be. This just thrills my heart as nothing else can.

He calls all of us. He calls you. If there is static on your line, ask him to clear it, so you can hear his voice. Then just do what he tells you to do and the doors to new life will open, I promise you.

If this little book helps just one person to understand the wonder of what God is offering us, then my efforts will be well worth it and I will be delighted.

If you knew Tesco's or Ralph's (USA) was giving away their food stocks, wouldn't you tell your friends, especially the hungry ones?

This is far bigger than that!

Why not knock on God's door? Why not venture inside his world and see for yourself? Why not?

IT IS AN AMAZING ADVENTURE!

One of my sons suggested I include here a few of the many testimonies people have given whose lives have been changed after taking Resurrected Life Ministry classes. Some of these people originally came for help or to see what RLM offers, many have now been trained to minister alongside with us. Here are some of their thoughts:

SAM . . .

"Even though I had four graduate degrees, including Theology and Psychology, something was terribly missing in my Christian walk of twenty years.

I was somehow unable to practically translate what I had learned, to overcome grave sins that desperately curtailed my Christian walk. Molly Sutherland's Resurrected Life Ministry classes helped traverse the longest distance in the universe—the ten inches from my head to deep within my heart.

Molly's approach purposely imitates Jesus' by combining teaching and demonstrating through ministry the miraculous power of the transforming love of Christ.

Because this approach so captivated me, I now boast that I am a 'recovering Psychotherapist' and have been a part of the RLM team ever since."

WOLFGANG . . .

"I came to RLM as someone who had a vast experience of all sorts of things in New Age. Before coming to RLM I knew Jesus superficially, and appreciated him as a good teacher, but I also carried a whole mixed bag of things with it, and thought that that was okay. I entered into a discipleship training program with Molly, which helped me to read and understand the Word of God, and experience inner healing and deliverance. I then started to maintain a new healthy life style with a personal relationship with God the Father, Jesus and the Holy Spirit, accepted accountability as an important factor in life and have never been happier. Thank you RLM for keeping me on the narrow path that leads to life."

LINDA ...

"RLM has been such a blessing in my Christian life. I have been a Christian for over thirty years. The first class has been transforming, because its primary purpose is to help everyone understand first and foremost who we are in Christ. Many of us try to perform for God, instead of learning first of all to be lovers of God, and to understand the amazing love he has for us. It is so exciting to watch people being ministered to, and to actually see them getting set free to love God in a deeper way."

BENJAMIN ...

"In RLM I have seen the love of God literally, tangibly dispelling fear, setting the captives free and breaking bondages, healing and delivering us his children so the world will know that God sent Jesus."

MARY ...

"I came to this class and it has been an amazing time. One word seems to sum it up, love; there has been so much love here, the love of God shared among us and love for each other. I have heard truths I have never really heard before, for instance I missed one session but read the literature that was given us entitled "My true worth and the lies that have distorted this truth." I read that we are not what we have, not what we feel, not what people say we are because we take our real identity from how God sees us: we are his child, who he loves. As I read this, suddenly I experienced his love for me and I knew how real this was. I also realized that I had been carrying for years a wrong version of myself. You see, I was the youngest of six children and had always been told, "She can't do that" and this had gone very deep in me so that in the end I believed it about myself. I felt inferior to my loving family, I was the one who could not do things right. As I read *My true worth,* I realized that this was not true, this was a lie. I had always known I was a child of God in my head, but suddenly I saw it clearly and it went into my heart and I really knew that God accepts and loves me. What a difference!

CHRISTOPHER ...

I became a Christian thirty-six years ago and it was as if I had been given a pack of cards which remained a pack. Molly is a facilitator, and it's as though she has taken the pack and opened it up and has shown me each card in turn.

Now I see that there is so much more to all this than I have ever known and I want more and more. Also the personal ministry that I received was wonderful and it has been life changing.

SARAH ...

God has moved so much in my life over the past five months since I started RLM. I came from a place of not knowing much about God, but I was looking for unconditional love and I found so much more than words can say.

God is showing me daily that when I let go of everything and hand it over to Jesus and ask the Holy Spirit to come into me to show me God's way, he does. It is not all about what God can do for me, but now I ask daily what is it that he would like me to do? Life is so much easier with God when I turn to him first with all my life's questions; and it's so lovely that I have started to hear God talking back to me with so much love and peace and I know that I am safe in his hands.

For example, God said to me, "Sarah, I can talk to everybody in the world, and when you have more of me in you than you have of yourself, you can talk to all the world just as I do."

MOLLY ...

Sarah told me that her 10 year-old son's class was asked by his teacher whether any of them believed in God. Sean's hand shot up and he answered that he definitely believed in God because God had just changed his mum so much, she was so happy now and so was he.

This is just a sample of testimonies people have written. I do have many, many more that evidence God's wonderful, healing, transforming love for us.

I hope this book has been of interest to you, and bless you for reading it. Why not pass it on to someone you know, otherwise books just gather dust don't they?

God bless you and your family now and always.

Molly.

(mollysutherland27@gmail.com)

POSTSCRIPT

I invite you to open your mind and join me and
read this poem or pray this prayer.

We really can make a difference!

We speak God's Kingdom to come as it is in Heaven for that is his will.

We speak his defeat of darkness, of death, of depression and dread.

With Jesus, we speak his Light, his Life, his Laughter, and his Love over our children, our homes, families and friends; over our hospitals, doctors and staff.

Light and Life and Laughter and Love over our farms, the factories and mills; over the mines, laboratories, business and shops, over our banks and trade.

Light and Life and Laughter and Love over our schools and all those who teach; over our churches, all pastors and priests.

Light and Life and Laughter and Love over our internet, TV, and phones; over our transport, cars, ships, trains and planes.

Light and Life and Laughter and Love over our prisons, our law-courts and police; over all accidents and those who assist.

Over our government, parliament too. Over our Queen, her family and staff; over the Forces, air, land and sea.

Light and Life and Laughter and Love over our country and God's wonderful world.

We can change the atmosphere over our land through our thoughts and prayers, for whatever we ask in union with God will be done. He has promised. So, with confidence we declare his Light, his Life, his Laughter and his Love to rule and reign in our lives and our land.

Thank you.

I would like to introduce to you our illustrator Kay Myregard.

It has been a real pleasure working closely with Kay Myregard to bring this book to you. Her illustrations are so important in conveying the message of the print. I have asked her to share something of herself with you.

She wrote:
"As a child I watched my mother paint landscapes when she could manage to find the time; it was her passion. Though little, I was one who watched, always aware. Many hours were spent in nature as I was driven to see even the smallest expression of life, always concocting and experimenting. Little did I know that my life was to be lived as an artist.
Educated at the California Institute of the Arts, with a BA in illustration, my life has happily been one of endless creating and effort mixed with unbridled curiosity.
I find my peace in dreaming, always with my eye on expanding my knowledge of God's creation and how to interpret my inner world into an actuality through my gift of art as my expression."

Thank you, Kay I am greatly indebted to you.

I would like to thank also my grandchildren who contributed their artistry in chapter three; my children who have given me advice and helpful feedback all along, and friends and RLM group members who have encouraged me in the writing of this book.

Lightning Source UK Ltd.
Milton Keynes UK
UKOW03f0029141113

220982UK00002B/56/P